New York State Legislature

Proceedings of the Senate and Assembly of the State of New York

ISBN/EAN: 9783744685085

Printed in Europe, USA, Canada, Australia, Japan

Cover: Foto ©Suzi / pixelio.de

More available books at **www.hansebooks.com**

New York State Legislature

Proceedings of the Senate and Assembly of the State of New York

In Memoriam.

ROSCOE CONKLING.

" He did not fall
Like drooping flowers that no man noticeth,
But like a great branch of some stately tree,
Rent in a tempest and flung down to death,
Thick with green leafage."   *   *   *   *

Proceedings

OF THE

SENATE AND ASSEMBLY

OF THE

State of New York,

IN RELATION TO THE DEATH OF

EX-SENATOR ROSCOE CONKLING,

HELD AT THE

CAPITOL, MAY 9, 1888.

ALBANY:
WEED, PARSONS AND COMPANY,
1889.

Proceedings

Legislature of the State of New York,

IN RELATION TO THE DEATH OF

Ex-Senator Roscoe Conkling.

In Assembly:

APRIL 18, 1888.

Mr. HUSTED, addressing the Chair, spoke as follows :

Mr. SPEAKER. — At fifty minutes after one this morning ROSCOE CONKLING passed away. When I make that statement I think this House will unanimously concur with me that we have a right to deviate from the usual course whereby we offer resolutions five minutes before the hour of adjournment.

I think this House will concur with me that a man so distinguished as he has been, that a man who has served this State so many years so faithfully and so well, who won for himself the first rank among Ameri-

can orators, American publicists and American statesmen, deserves especial consideration from the members
of the Legislature of the State of New York.

It is, sir, but nine years ago since, in this room, I
nominated him for Senator of the United States. I
did it then with pleasure and with pride. With grief
and sorrow I now announce his death, and I beg
leave, sir, to submit the following resolutions, which I
will read myself:

Resolved, That the Assembly learns with deep sorrow of the death
of Hon. ROSCOE CONKLING.

Resolved, That his distinguished public services, his high standard
of public honor, and his official and personal integrity, merit the
acknowledgment of the people of this State.

Resolved, That as Representative and Senator in Congress he won
the admiration of his colleagues and the plaudits of the Nation.

Resolved (if the Senate concur), That a joint committee, consisting
of five Senators and nine Members of the Assembly, be appointed
by the presiding officers of the respective Houses, to prepare a suitable memorial of the public services of the deceased orator and statesman, and to report to the Legislature what further action shall be
taken in order to pay to his memory the respectful tribute of their
sorrow.

Resolved, That out of respect to his memory this House do now
adjourn.

The resolutions, by a rising vote, were unanimously adopted.

In Memoriam.

In Senate:

Senator COGGESHALL offered the following:

Resolved, That the Senate of the State of New York learns with deep sorrow and profound regret of the death of the Hon. ROSCOE CONKLING. His long and distinguished services in Congress as a Representative and Senator from the State of New York, his great intellectual attainments and brilliant record, his honesty of public career and integrity, his loyalty of friendship and nobility of character, his illustrious and successful achievements, make his name and fame the common heritage of our State and Nation, and enshrine him in the hearts of the people.

Resolved (if the Assembly concur), That a committee of five Senators and nine Members of the Assembly be appointed by the President of the Senate and the Speaker of the Assembly to attend the funeral of Mr. CONKLING, and to make arrangements for appropriate memorial services by the Legislature.

Senators COGGESHALL, LOW and CANTOR spoke to the resolutions, and they were unanimously adopted by a rising vote.

The Assembly sent for concurrence the following resolutions:

Resolved, That the Assembly learns with deep sorrow of the death of Hon. ROSCOE CONKLING.

Resolved, That his distinguished public services, his high standard of public honor, and his official and personal integrity, merit the acknowledgment of the people of this State.

7

Resolved, That as a Republican Senator in Congress he has won the admiration of his colleagues and the plaudits of the Nation.

Resolved (if the Senate concur), That a joint committee, consisting of five Senators and nine Members of the Assembly, be appointed by the presiding officers of the respective Houses, to prepare a suitable memorial to the public services of the deceased orator and statesman, and to report to the Legislature what further action shall be taken in order to pay to his memory the respectful tribute of their sorrow; also,

Resolved (if the Senate concur), That a joint committee of nine Members of the Assembly and six Senators be appointed to attend the funeral of ROSCOE CONKLING.

The PRESIDENT. — The subject-matter of the resolutions sent by the Assembly has been already adopted by resolutions just introduced and passed in the Senate, and no action is necessary upon the resolutions of the Assembly.

Senator COGGESHALL said :

Mr. PRESIDENT.— It is not my purpose to pronounce any extended eulogy upon the character, life and services of the distinguished man whose death we so profoundly regret. No eulogies, no words of praise, no arch of victory, no monumental pile is needed to endear him to the people. The story of his useful and honorable life illumines the brightest pages of our history, and the fruits of his incessant labors, read and known of all men, give luster to his name and will perpetuate his memory. " He was a man, take him for all in all, we shall not look upon his like again;" a man of tireless activity and industry, and unsurpassed integrity in public, professional and private life.

In the councils of the Nation he bore a conspicuous and honorable part in the legislation necessary for the preservation and reconstruction of the Union, and is one of the most distinguished figures in our political history.

During nearly a quarter of a century of public service, when strong and brilliant men of both political parties fell, either by temptation or wicked and malicious denunciation, ROSCOE CONKLING'S fair fame and honor was untouched.

He was above alike corruption and suspicion. In an age when vituperation and calumny are the stock in trade of political warfare, he bore himself with such dignity and uprightness as to command the respect of all.

Although assailed and hounded and set upon by those who were jealous of his well-earned and richly-deserved success — although misrepresented, misjudged and wronged, and his proud, sensitive, high-spirited and chivalric soul wounded — yet the smell of fire was not on his garment.

All the shafts of malice fell idle and harmless against the impenetrable armor of uprightness and self-respect, with which he was fully panoplied.

He was above them all. He rested then, as now, "the knight without fear and without reproach," in the perpetual sunshine of an undying fame.

Sincere in his convictions, he despised shams and false pretense and hypocritical professions.

He thought for himself, and spoke what he thought. He was loyal to his own convictions. Friendship could not swerve him from the path of duty. Ambition could not tempt him. Enemies did not and could not daunt him. He was an open, honorable, manly foe; a loyal, true and constant friend. He never turned the back of his hand to a friend, nor his back to an enemy. He never "crooked the pregnant hinges of the knee that thrift might follow fawning." He never masqueraded. He was, as you saw him, the same at all times, in all places, and under all circumstances — the soul of honor.

> " Faithful found among the faithless.
> Unshaken, unseduced, unterrified;
> His loyalty kept, his love, his zeal,
> Nor number, nor example,
> With him wrought to swerve from truth,
> Or change his constant mind."

At the full meridian of intellectual greatness, with many years of usefulness and renown before him, at a time when, more than ever before, his magnificent leadership was required in the party of which he was so many years a conspicuous member, this great and good, honest, true and incorruptible man has closed his eyes in the dreamless sleep of death.

Why this must be is beyond human ken. Why this brave, strong, noble, lion-hearted man should go out from the activities and grand possibilities of a life such as his, and when he was so much needed by his party, his State and country, we know not.

To the stern decrees of an All-wise and Overruling Providence we bow with grief-stricken hearts. At the portals of his grave the whole civilized world mourns.

> "He did not fall
> Like drooping flowers that no man noticeth,
> But like a great branch of some stately tree,
> Rent in a tempest and flung down to death,
> Thick with green leafage — so that piteously
> Each passer by that ruin shuddereth,
> And saith, 'The gap this breach hath left is wide,
> The loss thereof can never be supplied.'"

As a born leader of men, as statesman or legislator, as lawyer, as citizen, as friend, we honor him and revere his memory.

To the loving and beloved wife and daughter, to his family, to the world, he has left a legacy greater, better and grander than earthly riches — a good name, a reputation untarnished, an integrity unimpaired; for, with Aristides, he could exclaim: "These are clean hands."

Senator Low said:

The Angel of Death has never taken a more kingly man, nor a more noble representative of all that is noblest and greatest in our civilization. I have known ROSCOE CONKLING well for the past thirty years; and among the great men who have honored their country and the world during that eventful period, he was the peer of the greatest and wisest and noblest of them all. He was a born leader of men, an intellectual giant; he never found his equal on the platform or in the arena of the Senate chamber. In his long service and public life he was free from all taint or suspicion of wrong or improper acts. He set an example well worthy of the imitation of the young men of the country. His loss will be long and keenly felt, and the mourning for his untimely taking off will be deep and lasting.

Senator CANTOR said:

I feel, Mr. President, that some expression of opinion should be given by those to whom ROSCOE CONKLING was politically opposed for so many years of his public life. The Democratic party, to which he was always so honorably opposed, and vigorously opposed, found in him an upright, an honorable, a consistent and a persistent political foe. He was of that class of men who rely absolutely upon his conviction of what was proper and right, upon principle. He always advocated from a consistency of purpose, and a direct manly belief that it was just and honorable. He was of that class of men, so rare in our community, who are governed absolutely by principle and conviction, and who rise, at times, higher than party exactions. The life of ROSCOE CONKLING was one that was fraught with great and noble deeds. As a Member of Congress he was a representative faithful to his trust, faithful to his people in the advocacy of all public measures which, in his judgment, redounded to the public benefit. Faithful in all respects. His

---

services will be forever recognized and appreciated, not only by the people of the district which he so well represented, and by the people of the State whose Senator he was for two terms in the Senate of the United States; but, sir, he has found a place in the hearts of all the people who believe that honesty of purpose and devotion to country rise paramount to all other considerations. I heartily second the adoption of the resolution.

Senator COGGESHALL offered the following:

Resolved, As a token of respect to the memory of the deceased, that the Senate do now adjourn.

The resolution was adopted.

In Assembly:

APRIL 19, 1888.

Mr. BEATTY offered the following resolution:

Resolved (if the Senate concur), That a joint committee of nine Members of the Assembly and six Senators be appointed to attend the funeral of Hon. ROSCOE CONKLING.

The resolution was unanimously adopted.

In Senate:

APRIL 19, 1888.

Senator COGGESHALL offered the following:

WHEREAS, The funeral of the Hon. ROSCOE CONKLING will occur in the city of New York on Friday, the twentieth instant; and

WHEREAS, His distinguished services in public life and his great eminence as a statesman, call for a marked expression of the high esteem in which he was held by the people of the State, therefore, be it

Resolved (if the Assembly concur), That when the Senate and Assembly adjourn this evening, it be until Monday evening at a quarter past eight o'clock.

The PRESIDENT put the question, and the resolution was adopted.

The PRESIDENT announced the following committees, pursuant to the concurrent resolutions of the Senate and Assembly, to attend the funeral of the Hon. ROSCOE CONKLING, and to make arrangements for appropriate memorial services by the Legislature: Senators COGGESHALL, LEWIS, SWEET, LAUGHLIN, MURPHY and REILLY; also, to attend the funeral in the city of New York: Senators COGGESHALL, SWEET, VAN COTT, O'CONNOR, CANTOR and STADLER.

The Assembly returned the resolution relative

to the death of the Hon. ROSCOE CONKLING, with a message that they had concurred in the passage of the same without amendment, and had appointed as a committee on the part of the House, Messrs. HUSTED, GALLAGHER, HUNTTING, ENZ, BEATTY, BLUMENTHAL, JOHN MARTIN, GORDON and KENT.

In Assembly:

APRIL 19, 1888.

The Senate sent for concurrence the following resolutions:

Resolved, That the Senate of the State of New York learns with deep sorrow and profound regret of the death of the Hon. ROSCOE CONKLING. His long and distinguished services in Congress as a Representative and Senator from the State of New York, his great intellectual attainments and brilliant record, his honesty of public career and integrity, his loyalty of friendship and nobility of character, his illustrious and successful achievements, make his name and fame the common heritage of our State and Nation, and enshrine him in the hearts of the people.

Resolved (if the Senate concur), That a committee of five Senators and nine Members of the Assembly be appointed by the President of the Senate and the Speaker of the Assembly to attend the funeral of Mr. CONKLING, and to make arrangements for appropriate memorial services by the Legislature.

The resolutions were unanimously adopted.

Legislative Proceedings.

The SPEAKER announced the following committee to attend the funeral of the Hon. ROSCOE CONKLING and to draft resolutions: Mr. HUSTED, Mr. GALLAGHER, Mr. HUNTTING, Mr. ENZ, Mr. BEATTY, Mr. BLUMENTHAL, Mr. JOHN MARTIN, Mr. GORDON and Mr. KENT.

The Senate sent for concurrence the following resolution:

WHEREAS, The funeral of the Hon. ROSCOE CONKLING will occur in the city of New York on Friday, the twentieth instant; and

WHEREAS, His distinguished services in public life and his great eminence as a statesman, call for a marked expression of the esteem with which he was held by the people of this State, therefore, be it

Resolved (if the Assembly concur), That when the Senate and Assembly adjourn this evening, it be until Monday evening next at a quarter past eight o'clock.

The resolution was adopted.

In Memoriam.

In Assembly:

The Senate sent for concurrence a resolution in the words following:

Resolved (if the Assembly concur), That a joint committee having in charge the exercises in memory of the late ROSCOE CONKLING, be requested to invite to attend the exercises the members of the present Congress, and such members of preceding sessions as sat in the House or Senate with Mr. CONKLING.

The resolution was adopted.

Proceedings in Joint Session

OF THE

SENATE AND ASSEMBLY.

Academy of Music:

MAY 9, 1888.

The Legislature having met in Joint Session at the Academy of Music, in the city of Albany, in pursuance of arrangements made by the Joint Memorial Committee, the Hon. EDWARD F. JONES, Lieutenant-Governor and President of the Senate, in the Chair, on calling the assemblage to order, said:

It is of ROSCOE CONKLING we would speak. Not in words of praise, for none that we could utter would place him higher in the estimation of his countrymen, for his fame now perches on the highest pinnacle of renown.

Not in tones of affection, for the tender language of love is the sacred property of those nearer and dearer to him than we, who only knew him as a public man, can ever be.

Our language is inspired by higher emotions. It is with tributes of respect that we would humbly endow his memory.

When death claims as its victim an honored statesman, the prejudices of partisanship fade away, and in this instance, we not only remember that the man was great, but that he honored his greatness with his character, and all hasten to reverence his virtues. We meet on this occasion and vie each with the other in strewing his grave with never-fading flowers. We assemble this evening for the purpose of embalming his memory with tributes of eloquence.

The Committee having the arrangements in charge, have wisely selected to perform this duty, the one who could do it best, ROSCOE CONKLING'S friend, the Hon. ROBERT G. INGERSOLL, whom it is my privilege to present to you.

𝕸𝖊𝖒𝖔𝖗𝖎𝖆𝖑 𝕬𝖉𝖉𝖗𝖊𝖘𝖘

ON

ROSCOE CONKLING

BY

𝕽𝖔𝖇𝖊𝖗𝖙 𝕲. 𝕴𝖓𝖌𝖊𝖗𝖘𝖔𝖑𝖑,

DELIVERED BEFORE THE

New York State Legislature, at Albany, N. Y.

Memorial Address.

Roscoe Conkling — a great man, an orator, a statesman, a lawyer, a distinguished citizen of the Republic, in the zenith of his fame and power has reached his journey's end; and we are met, here in the city of his birth, to pay our tribute to his worth and work. He earned and held a proud position in the public thought. He stood for independence, for courage, and above all for absolute integrity, and his name was known and honored by many millions of his fellow men.

The literature of many lands is rich with the tributes that gratitude, admiration and love have paid to the great and honored dead. These tributes disclose the character of nations, the ideals of the human race. In them we find the estimates of greatness—the deeds and lives that challenged praise and thrilled the hearts of men.

In the presence of death, the good man judges as he would be judged. He knows that men are only fragments — that the greatest walk in shadow, and that faults and failures mingle with the lives of all.

In the grave should be buried the prejudices and passions born of conflict. Charity should hold the scales in which are weighed the deeds of men. Peculiarities, traits born of locality and surroundings — these are but the dust of the race — these are accidents, drapery, clothes, fashions, that have nothing to do with the man except to hide his character. They are the clouds that cling to mountains. Time gives us clearer vision. That which was merely local fades away. The words of envy are forgotten, and all there is of sterling worth remains. He who was called a partisan is a patriot. The revolutionist and the outlaw are the founders of nations, and he who was regarded as a scheming, selfish politician becomes a statesman, a philosopher, whose words and deeds shed light.

Fortunate is that nation great enough to know the great. When a great man dies—one who has nobly fought the battle of a life, who has been faithful to every trust, and has uttered his highest, noblest thought—one who has stood proudly by the right in spite of jeer and taunt, neither stopped by foe nor swerved by friend—in honoring him, in speaking words of praise and love above his dust, we pay a tribute to ourselves.

How poor this world would be without its graves, without the memories of its mighty dead. Only the voiceless speak forever.

Intelligence, integrity and courage are the great pillars that support the State.

Above all, the citizens of a free nation should honor the brave and independent man—the man of stainless integrity, of will and intellectual force. Such men are the Atlases on whose mighty shoulders rest the great fabric of the republic. Flatterers, cringers, crawlers, time-servers are the dangerous citizens of a democracy. They who gain applause and power by pandering to the mistakes, the prejudices and passions of the multitude, are the enemies of liberty.

When the intelligent submit to the clamor of the many, anarchy begins and the republic reaches the edge of chaos. Mediocrity, touched with ambition, flatters the base and calumniates the great, while the true patriot, who will do neither, is often sacrificed.

In a government of the people a leader should be a teacher — he should carry the torch of truth.

Most people are the slaves of habit — followers of custom — believers in the wisdom of the past—and were it not for brave and splendid souls, "the dust of antique time would lie unswept, and mountainous error be too highly heaped for truth to overpeer." Custom is a prison, locked and barred by those who long ago were dust, the keys of which are in the keeping of the dead.

Nothing is grander than when a strong, intrepid man breaks chains, levels walls and breasts the many-headed mob like some great cliff that meets and mocks the innumerable billows of the sea.

The politician hastens to agree with the majority—insists that their prejudice is patriotism, that their ignorance is wisdom;—not that he loves them, but because he loves

himself. The statesman, the real
reformer, points out the mistakes of
the multitude, attacks the prejudices
of his countrymen, laughs at their
follies, denounces their cruelties, en-
lightens and enlarges their minds
and educates the conscience — not
because he loves himself, but because he loves and serves the right
and wishes to make his country
great and free.

With him defeat is but a spur to
further effort. He who refuses to
stoop, who cannot be bribed by the
promise of success, or the fear of fail-
ure — who walks the highway of the
right, and in disaster stands erect,
is the only victor. Nothing is more
despicable than to reach fame by
crawling, — position by cringing.

When real history shall be writ-

ten by the truthful and the wise,
these men, these kneelers at the
shrines of chance and fraud, these
brazen idols worshipped once as
gods, will be the very food of scorn,
while those who bore the burden of
defeat, who earned and kept their
self-respect, who would not bow to
man or men for place or power, will
wear upon their brows the laurel
mingled with the oak.

ROSCOE CONKLING was a man of
superb courage.

He not only acted without fear,
but he had that fortitude of soul
that bears the consequences of the
course pursued without complaint.
He was charged with being proud.
The charge was true—he was proud.
His knees were as inflexible as the
"unwedgeable and gnarled oak," but

he was not vain. Vanity rests on the opinion of others—pride, on our own. The source of vanity is from without—of pride, from within. Vanity is a vane that turns, a willow that bends, with every breeze—pride is the oak that defies the storm. One is cloud—the other rock. One is weakness—the other strength.

This imperious man entered public life in the dawn of the reformation—at a time when the country needed men of pride, of principle and courage. The institution of slavery had poisoned all the springs of power. Before this crime ambition fell upon its knees,—politicians, judges, clergymen, and merchant-princes bowed low and humbly, with their hats in their hands.

The real friend of man was denounced as the enemy of his country—the real enemy of the human race was called a statesman and a patriot. Slavery was the bond and pledge of peace, of union, and national greatness. The temple of American liberty was finished—the auction-block was the corner-stone.

It is hard to conceive of the utter demoralization, of the political blindness and immorality, of the patriotic dishonesty, of the cruelty and degradation of a people who supplemented the incomparable Declaration of Independence with the Fugitive Slave Law.

Think of the honored statesmen of that ignoble time who wallowed in this mire, and who, decorated with dripping filth, received the plaudits of their fellow-men. The noble, the really patriotic, were the victims of mobs, and the shameless were clad in the robes of office.

But let us speak no word of blame—let us feel that each one acted according to his light—according to his darkness.

At last the conflict came. The hosts of light and darkness prepared to meet upon the fields of war. The question was presented: Shall the Republic be slave or free? The Republican party had triumphed at the polls. The greatest man in our history was President elect. The victors were appalled—they shrank from the great responsibility of success. In the presence of rebellion they hesitated —they offered to return the fruits

of victory. Hoping to avert war
they were willing that slavery should
become immortal. An amendment
to the Constitution was proposed, to
the effect that no subsequent amendment should ever be made that in
any way should interfere with the
right of man to steal his fellow-men.

This, the most marvelous propo-
sition ever submitted to a Congress
of civilized men, received in the
House an overwhelming majority,
and the necessary two-thirds in the
Senate. The Republican party, in
the moment of its triumph, deserted
every principle for which it had so
gallantly contended, and with the
trembling hands of fear laid its convictions on the altar of compromise.

The Old Guard, numbering but
sixty-five in the House, stood as

firm as the three hundred at Ther-
mopylæ. Thaddeus Stevens — as
maliciously right as any other man
was ever wrong — refused to kneel.
Owen Lovejoy, remembering his
brother's noble blood, refused to
surrender, and on the edge of dis-
union, in the shadow of civil war,
with the air filled with sounds of
dreadful preparation, while the Republican party was retracing its
steps, ROSCOE CONKLING voted No.
This puts a wreath of glory on his
tomb. From that vote to the last
moment of his life he was a cham-
pion of equal rights, stanch and
stalwart.

From that moment he stood in
the front rank. He never wavered
and he never swerved. By his devotion to principle — his courage,

the splendor of his diction,—by his varied and profound knowledge, his conscientious devotion to the great cause, and by his intellectual scope and grasp, he won and held the admiration of his fellow-men.

Disasters in the field, reverses at the polls, did not and could not shake his courage or his faith. He knew the ghastly meaning of defeat. He knew that the great ship that slavery sought to strand and wreck was freighted with the world's sublimest hope.

He battled for a nation's life— for the rights of slaves—the dignity of labor, and the liberty of all. He guarded with a father's care the rights of the hunted, the hated and despised. He attacked the savage statutes of the reconstructed States with a torrent of invective, scorn and execration. He was not satisfied until the freedman was an American Citizen — clothed with every civil right — until the Constitution was his shield — until the ballot was his sword.

And long after we are dead, the colored man in this and other lands will speak his name in reverence and love. Others wavered, but he stood firm; some were false, but he was proudly true — fearlessly faithful unto death.

He gladly, proudly grasped the hands of colored men who stood with him as makers of our laws, and treated them as equals and as friends. The cry of "social equality" coined and uttered by the cruel and the base, was to him the expression of a great and splendid truth. He knew that no man can be the equal of one he robs—that the intelligent and unjust are not the superiors of the ignorant and honest—and he also felt, and proudly felt, that if he were not too great to reach the hand of help and recognition to the slave, no other Senator could rightfully refuse.

We rise by raising others—and he who stoops above the fallen, stands erect.

Nothing can be grander than to sow the seeds of noble thoughts and virtuous deeds—to liberate the bodies and the souls of men—to earn the grateful homage of a race— and then, in life's last shadowy hour, to know that the historian of Liberty will be compelled to write your name.

38

There are no words intense enough,
—with heart enough—to express
my admiration for the great and
gallant souls who have in every age
and every land upheld the right,
and who have lived and died for
freedom's sake.

In our lives have been the grand-
est years that man has lived, that
Time has measured by the flight
of worlds.

The history of that great Party
that let the oppressed go free—that
lifted our nation from the depths
of savagery to freedom's cloudless
heights, and tore with holy hands
from every law the words that sanc-
tified the cruelty of man, is the
most glorious in the annals of our
race. Never before was there such
a moral exaltation—never a party

with a purpose so pure and high.
It was the embodied conscience of
a nation, the enthusiasm of a people guided by wisdom, the imper-
sonation of justice; and the sub-
lime victory achieved loaded even
the conquered with all the rights
that freedom can bestow.

ROSCOE CONKLING was an absolutely honest man.

Honesty is the oak around which
all other virtues cling. Without
that they fall, and groveling die in
weeds and dust. He believed that
a nation should discharge its obligations. He knew that a promise
could not be made often enough, or
emphatic enough, to take the place
of payment. He felt that the promise of the government was the promise of every citizen—that a national

obligation was a personal debt, and that no possible combination of words and pictures could take the place of coin. He uttered the splendid truth that "the higher obligations among men are not set down in writing signed and sealed, but reside in honor." He knew that repudiation was the sacrifice of honor — the death of the national soul. He knew that without character, without integrity, there is no wealth, and that below poverty, below bankruptcy, is the rayless abyss of repudiation. He upheld the sacredness of contracts, of plighted national faith, and helped to save and keep the honor of his native land. This adds another laurel to his brow.

He was the ideal representative,

faithful and incorruptible. He believed that his constituents and his country were entitled to the fruit of his experience, to his best and highest thought. No man ever held the standard of responsibility higher than he. He voted according to his judgment, his conscience. He made no bargains — he neither bought nor sold.

To correct evils, abolish abuses and inaugurate reforms, he believed was not only the duty, but the privilege, of a legislator. He neither sold nor mortgaged himself. He was in Congress during the years of vast expenditure, of war and waste—when the credit of the nation was loaned to individuals— when claims were thick as leaves in June, when the amendment of a statute, the change of a single word, meant millions, and when empires were given to corporations. He stood at the summit of his power— peer of the greatest—a leader tried and trusted. He had the tastes of a prince, the fortune of a peasant, and yet he never swerved. No corporation was great enough or rich enough to purchase him. His vote could not be bought "for all the sun sees, or the close earth wombs, or the profound seas hide." His hand was never touched by any bribe, and on his soul there never was a sordid stain. Poverty was his priceless crown.

Above his marvelous intellectual gifts—above all place he ever reached,—above the ermine he refused,—rises his integrity like some great mountain peak—and there it stands, firm as the earth beneath, pure as the stars above.

He was a great lawyer. He understood the frame-work, the anatomy, the foundations of law; was familiar with the great streams and currents and tides of authority.

He knew the history of legislation—the principles that have been settled upon the fields of war. He knew the maxims,—those crystallizations of common sense, those hand-grenades of argument. He was not a case-lawyer—a decision index, or an echo; he was original, thoughtful and profound. He had breadth and scope, resource, learning, logic, and above all, a sense of justice. He was painstaking and conscientious—anxious to know the facts—

preparing for every attack, ready for every defense. He rested only when the end was reached. During the contest, he neither sent nor received a flag of truce. He was true to his clients—making their case his. Feeling responsibility, he listened patiently to details, and to his industry there were only the limits of time and strength. He was a student of the Constitution. He knew the boundaries of State and Federal jurisdiction, and no man was more familiar with those great decisions that are the peaks and promontories, the headlands and the beacons, of the law.

He was an orator,—earnest, logical, intense and picturesque. He laid the foundation with care, with accuracy and skill, and rose by "cold gradation and well-balanced form" from the corner-stone of statement to the domed conclusion. He filled the stage. He satisfied the eye—the audience was his. He had that indefinable thing called presence. Tall, commanding, erect —ample in speech, graceful in compliment, Titanic in denunciation, rich in illustration, prodigal of comparison and metaphor—and his sentences, measured and rhythmical, fell like music on the enraptured throng.

He abhorred the Pharisee, and loathed all conscientious fraud. He had a profound aversion for those who insist on putting base motives back of the good deeds of others. He wore no mask. He knew his friends—his enemies knew him.

He had no patience with pretense — with patriotic reasons for unmanly acts. He did his work and bravely spoke his thought.

Sensitive to the last degree, he keenly felt the blows and stabs of the envious and obscure — of the smallest, of the weakest — but the greatest could not drive him from conviction's field. He would not stoop to ask or give an explanation. He left his words and deeds to justify themselves.

He held in light esteem a friend who heard with half-believing ears the slander of a foe. He walked a highway of his own, and kept the company of his self-respect. He would not turn aside to avoid a foe — to greet or gain a friend.

In his nature there was no com-

promise. To him there were but
two paths—the right and wrong.
He was maligned, misrepresented
and misunderstood—but he would
not answer. He knew that character speaks louder far than any
words. He was as silent then as
he is now—and his silence, better
than any form of speech, refuted
every charge.

He was an American—proud of
his country, that was and ever will
be proud of him. He did not find
perfection only in other lands. He
did not grow small and shrunken,
withered and apologetic, in the presence of those upon whom greatness
had been thrust by chance. He
could not be overawed by dukes or
lords, nor flattered into vertebrate-
less subserviency by the patronizing

smiles of kings. In the midst of
conventionalities he had the feeling
of suffocation. He believed in the
royalty of man, in the sovereignty
of the citizen, and in the matchless
greatness of this Republic.

He was of the classic mould —
a figure from the antique world.
He had the pose of the great stat-
ues—the pride and bearing of the
intellectual Greek, of the conquering
Roman, and he stood in the wide
free air, as though within his veins
there flowed the blood of a hundred
kings.

And as he lived he died. Proudly
he entered the darkness — or the
dawn — that we call death. Un-
shrinkingly he passed beyond our
horizon, beyond the twilight's pur-
ple hills, beyond the utmost reach

49

of human harm or help—to that vast realm of silence or of joy where the innumerable dwell, and he has left with us his wealth of thought and deed—the memory of a brave, imperious, honest man, who bowed alone to death.

Mr. HUSTED said:

Mr. CHAIRMAN.—I move that the thanks of the Legislature be tendered to the Hon. ROBERT G. INGERSOLL, for the masterly oration to which we have listened, and, sir, in making this motion, I am confident that I express the unanimous sentiment of this body, when I say that in purity of style, in poetic expression, in cogency of statement and brilliancy of rhetoric it stands unrivaled among the eulogies of either ancient or modern days. As effective as Demosthenes, as polished as Cicero, as ornate as Burke, as scholarly as Gladstone, the orator of the evening, in surpassing others, has eclipsed himself.

Senator COGGESHALL said:

Mr. CHAIRMAN. - No words that I can utter

will add to the able and eloquent eulogy pronounced by Mr. INGERSOLL upon the life, character and services of ROSCOE CONKLING.

It is indeed a worthy tribute by one of America's most gifted orators to one of the foremost men of his time.

On behalf of the Senate and Assembly, I second the motion of the gentleman from Westchester.

CONCURRENT RESOLUTIONS.

In Assembly:

January 17, 1889.

Resolved (if the Senate concur), That there be printed under the direction of the Clerks of the Senate and Assembly, four thousand (4,000) copies of the proceedings of the Legislature and the memorial oration of Col. Robert G. Ingersoll, on the death of ex-Senator ROSCOE CONKLING, for the use of the members of the Legislature, and one thousand (1,000) copies for the officers and reporters, to be distributed by the Clerks of each House.

By order of the Assembly,

C. A. CHICKERING, *Clerk.*

STATE OF NEW YORK:
In Assembly, *January 18, 1889.*
The amendments of the Senate duly concurred in,
By order of the Assembly,
C. A. CHICKERING,
Clerk.

STATE OF NEW YORK:
In Senate, *January 18, 1889.*
Passed with the following amendment:
Strike out "1,000" and insert "3,000."
Strike out "1,000" and insert "2,000."
By order of the Senate,
JOHN S. KENYON,
Clerk.

In Senate:

January 18, 1889.

Resolved (if the Assembly concur), That of the 8,000 extra copies of the CONKLING MEMORIAL ordered printed, that 1,000 copies be distributed to the State officers.

STATE OF NEW YORK:
In Assembly, *January 21, 1889.*
Concurred in without amendment,
By order of the Assembly,
C. A. CHICKERING,
Clerk.

STATE OF NEW YORK:
In Senate, *January 18, 1889.*
The foregoing resolution was passed.
By order of the Senate,
JOHN S. KENYON,
Clerk.